# LIFE IN A DECIDUOUS FOREST

# LIFE IN A DECIDUOUS FOREST

DIANNE M. MACMILLAN

Lerner Publications Company
Minneapolis

With heartfelt thanks the author wishes to acknowledge Ruth Shaw Radlauer for her guidance, encouragement, and friendship; the Adirondack Mountain Club (ADK) for their continued commitment to environmental education and conservation of our natural resources; Joe Racete and Jim Conley from the New York State Department of Environmental Conservation; and Deborah L. Stout, Director of The Adirondack Teacher Center.

Lerner Publications Company
A division of Lerner Publishing Group
241 First Avenue North
Minneapolis, MN 55401 U.S.A.

Website address: www.lernerbooks.com


Library of Congress Cataloging-in-Publication Data

MacMillan, Dianne M., 1943–
    Life in a deciduous forest / by Dianne M. MacMillan.
       p.   cm. — (Ecosystems in action)
    Summary: Explores the Adirondack forests of New York state, discussing how the forest develops, the plants and animals found there, and ways in which the living and nonliving parts of the forest work together.
Includes bibliographic references and index.
   ISBN: 0–8225–4684–1 (lib. bdg. : alk. paper)
   1. Forest ecology—New York (State)—Adirondack Mountains—Juvenile literature. [1. Forests—New York (State) 2. Forest ecology. 3. Ecology. 4. Adirondack Mountains (N.Y.)] I. Title. II. Series.
QH105.N7 M33 2003
577.3'09747'5—dc21                            2002013953

Manufactured in the United States of America
1 2 3 4 5 6 – JR – 08 07 06 05 04 03

# CONTENTS

# WHAT IS AN ECOSYSTEM?

Biomes are particular types of living communities of plants and animals. These communities are characterized by one dominant type of vegetation. Examples of biomes found on land are deserts, forests, grasslands, and tundra. Each biome has a unique climate and yearly patterns of rainfall and sunlight as well as certain kinds of soil.

Within each biome, there are smaller units, called ecosystems, composed of biotic (living) and abiotic (physical) parts. The biotic parts are the plants, animals, fungi, and bacteria. The abiotic parts are the minerals and nutrients found in the soil, along with temperature and precipitation, that make up the environment or habitat. The living and nonliving parts of an ecosystem interact. The living things are dependent upon one another and the environment for their existence. A constant exchange of matter and energy creates a natural balance.

All living things need energy to live. Most of this energy comes from the sun. Trees and green plants turn sunlight into food, or chemical energy, in a process called photosynthesis. During photosynthesis chlorophyll, the green pigment found in leaves, enables plants to combine carbon dioxide from the air with water from the soil to make glucose, a form of sugar. The glucose supplies the energy plants need to grow stems, leaves, flowers, fruit, and seeds. Each part of the plant contains this stored chemical energy. When an animal eats a plant, the stored energy from sunlight is passed on to that animal. If, in turn, that animal is eaten by another animal, the energy travels to the new animal.

Trees and plants are the primary producers of energy in a food chain. Herbivores (plant eaters, such as caterpillars and squirrels) are primary consumers. They cannot make their own food and must obtain energy by eating leaves, acorns, and other parts of plants. Carnivores (flesh eaters), are secondary consumers, or animals that eat plant eaters. Carnivores include predators such as hawks, owls, coyotes, and bobcats. Predators help keep the ecosystem balanced. Some carnivores are scavengers, which means they feed on the dead remains of animals. Scavengers include birds, such as ravens, and small mammals, such as martens and fishers. They help keep the ecosystem clean. Dead plants and animals also become food for hosts of other smaller organisms called decomposers. Decomposers such as millipedes, earthworms, mites, springtails, fungi, and microscopic bacteria complete the food cycle by consuming the dead tissue and reducing it to small particles of

nutrients and minerals such as nitrogen, carbon, iron, and hydrogen. These minerals and nutrients in the soil are absorbed by plant roots and transported, along with water, to the leaves, where photosynthesis takes place, completing the food cycle.

Forests are among the most densely populated places on earth. Each tree supports a variety of smaller plants, animals, and microscopic organisms. There are four forest biomes found in the temperate climate zone, the part of the Northern Hemisphere between the Tropic of Cancer and the Arctic Circle. These types are deciduous forests, evergreen forests, forests with mixed deciduous and evergreen trees, and rain forests.

A deciduous forest is made up primarily of trees that lose all their leaves once a year. The leaves of a

**FORESTS ARE AMONG THE MOST DENSELY POPULATED PLACES ON EARTH. EACH TREE SUPPORTS A VARIETY OF SMALLER PLANTS, ANIMALS, AND MICROSCOPIC ORGANISMS.**

deciduous tree are flat, wide, and soft. Deciduous trees are also called broadleaf or hardwood trees. They all produce flowers, and after pollination, the flowers develop seeds. The seeds may grow inside hard nuts like walnuts or acorns, or inside pods, berries, or fleshy fruits such as apples or pears. Seeds fall to the ground when ripe or are carried by the wind to other areas. Some are propelled by "wings," such as those on the seeds of sugar maple, elm, or ash trees.

In contrast, trees in an evergreen or coniferous forest keep their leaves, sometimes for as long as five years. Leaves on coniferous trees are long and slender like pine needles or short and pointed like spruce needles. Seeds grow in tight spirals inside cones.

Most deciduous trees grow in climates with four distinct seasons. Winter temperatures may be below freezing, while summers are warm and humid. Shutting down photosynthesis and losing leaves in autumn is the way deciduous

**LEAVES OF A RED MAPLE**
*(ACER RUBRUM)*

**NEEDLES OF AN EASTERN WHITE PINE**
*(PINUS STROBUS)*

trees adapt to cold temperatures. Deciduous forests receive 30 to 80 inches (80 to 200 centimeters) of precipitation a year in the form of rain, sleet, snow, and hail. Only rain forests receive more moisture than deciduous forests.

Deciduous forests are found mostly in the Northern Hemisphere, in parts of North America and across Europe and Asia. Deciduous trees flourished in these areas about 100 million years ago. Then, during the Ice Age, which began 1.8 million years ago, advancing sheets of ice destroyed the northernmost stands of trees. Ten thousand years ago, the ice retreated and broadleaf trees moved back into the northern areas. Deciduous forests expanded to cover areas in western Europe and eastern Asia, and areas in eastern North America from the Great Lakes south to the Gulf of Mexico and from the Atlantic Ocean west to the Mississippi River. In this book we will explore life in a deciduous forest in the Adirondack Mountains, in the state of New York.

**WINTER SNOW HELPS STRIP DEAD BROWN LEAVES FROM DECIDUOUS TREES** (LEFT SIDE OF PHOTO). **CONIFEROUS TREES** (RIGHT) **KEEP THEIR NEEDLES IN SPITE OF HEAVY ACCUMULATIONS OF SNOW.**

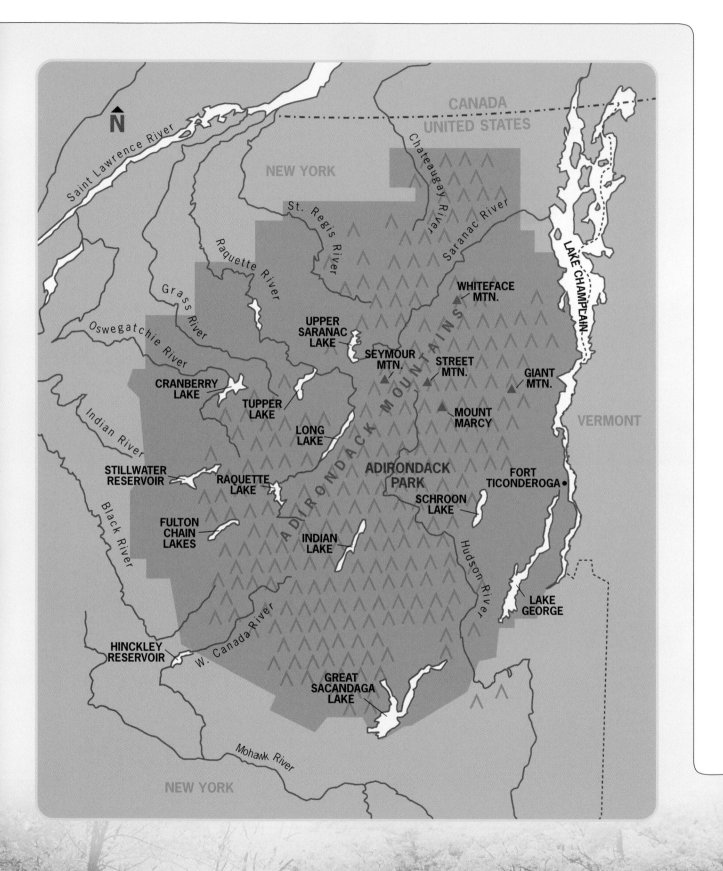

# CHAPTER 1

# THE DECIDUOUS FOREST IN THE ADIRONDACKS

The Adirondack region covers about one-third of the land area of New York State. It is bounded on the north by the St. Lawrence River Valley, on the east by Lake Champlain, and on the south by the Mohawk River Valley. Forty-three mountain peaks in the area are more than 4,000 feet (1,200 meters) high.

More than one billion years ago, magma—molten rock from deep within the earth's crust—rose to the surface, where it cooled to form metamorphic rock. The rock was pushed up into a mountain range that was higher than Mt. Everest, which is 29,035 feet (8,850 m tall). Over the next five hundred million years, water and wind eroded

(stripped away) most of this rock, leveling the land. Shallow seas invaded then, depositing thick layers of sand and mud that over the ages were compressed into sedimentary rock. Then an area of magma from deep within the earth rose under the Adirondack region. It pushed on the earth's crust and expanded it upward into a

**THE ADIRONDACK MOUNTAINS LIE WEST OF LAKE CHAMPLAIN** (FRONT).

massive dome of mountains. Most mountain ranges, such as the Rocky Mountains and the Appalachians, are long strips of mountainous areas. The Adirondack dome is the only circular mountain mass found within the United States. The dome is 160 miles (260 km) wide and 1 mile (1.6 km) high. Over the ages, the softer sedimentary rock eroded, exposing the ancient metamorphic rock that had been pushed up from the earth's crust. Geologists sometimes refer to the Adirondacks as "new mountains from old rocks."

About 350 million years ago, tree ferns and spiky club mosses began to grow in the area. Cone-bearing evergreen trees replaced them about 240 million years ago. Slowly over time, flowering plants and deciduous trees made their appearance, and by 10 million years ago, they were flourishing.

MOST MOUNTAIN RANGES, SUCH AS THE ROCKY MOUNTAINS AND THE APPALACHIANS, TAKE THE FORM OF LONG BANDS OF MOUNTAINOUS AREAS. THE ADIRONDACK DOME IS THE ONLY CIRCULAR MOUNTAIN MASS FOUND WITHIN THE UNITED STATES.

Then, 1.5 million years ago, glaciers (huge sheets of ice) moved over the region. Glaciers advanced and receded at least four times. The last glacier receded from the Adirondack region about ten thousand years ago. Glaciers left a landscape of gouged-out valleys, more than 2,800 lakes and ponds, and 6,000 miles (10,000 km) of rivers and streams that flow out from the Adirondack Mountains in a radial pattern, like spokes on a wheel. Glaciers also left glacial debris, called till. This unsorted mixture of clay, silt, sand, gravel, and boulders was formed beneath and within glaciers. Rocks were carried and ground up by the flowing ice. As the glaciers melted, till was left behind on the land. The rocks in the till are often rough and jagged. Till may be found as a thin covering on mountaintops or as thicker layers of stony debris at lower elevations.

Adirondack waters drain from the central part of the dome eastward to Lake Champlain, northward to the St. Lawrence River, westward to Lake Ontario, and southward to the Hudson and Mohawk Rivers. Water flows in an endless cycle through the landscape. It is continually replenished by flakes of snow, drops of rain and dew, and moisture collected into clouds and fog. This moisture is necessary to maintain the forest ecosystem.

## PLANT SUCCESSION

With the glaciers gone, warmer temperatures allowed plant and animal species from the south and west to move back into their former territories. Some of the glacial till washed off the summits and high ridges, leaving bare rock where lichens and mosses began to grow. In time, grass and then small shrubs grew, including dwarf birch, alpine bilberry, crowberry, and mountain alder. Next, conifer species such as white spruce and balsam fir arrived. After another thousand years, the first broad-leaved, or

**RUNNING CLUB MOSS (*LYCOPODIUM CLAVATUM*)**

deciduous, trees began to grow at lower elevations. As the climate warmed, more and more varieties of deciduous trees arrived in the region. Yellow birch, elm, sugar maple, and American beech became the most common.

Scientists call this gradual replacement of one community of plants by another over a period of time succession. A succession of plant communities is always accompanied by a succession of animal communities. Plant succession leads the way because plants are the foundation of every food chain. After centuries, a self-sustaining, long-lasting community of organisms reaches the climax, or final stage, of development.

A climax forest is a stable forest community. It is in natural balance with the environment. A climax forest may last for thousands of years unless the environment is disturbed by a major event—such as a strong windstorm, a change in climate, disease, or a fire—that kills the trees.

After a disturbance occurs, seeds of pioneer species take advantage of the newly open ground and sunlight. Quaking aspen and paper birch have light seeds that can be carried by the wind far from the mother tree, making them readily available to start new forests. Seeds of the fire cherry tree are scattered by bird droppings, with ready-made fertilizer to help them get started. Some seeds, including raspberries, may remain in the soil for decades, awaiting a disturbance to the forest.

Pioneer plants can withstand harsh environmental conditions, such as poor soil, full sunlight, and wide variations in temperature and moisture. As they establish themselves, they alter the area's conditions by adding organic matter to the soil and by shading it. This helps the soil to retain moisture.

As conditions improve, different plants that are better adapted to the improved conditions are able to move into the area. The original pioneer plants, shaded by new taller trees, slow their growth and die. Pioneer plants are found only in open areas, and most will vanish from the colonized site in about seventy years.

# SUCCESSION IN A DECIDUOUS FOREST

1. FOLLOWING A DISTURBANCE, SHADE INTOLERANT PIONEERING PLANTS GROW IN A CLEARING.

2. MID-TOLERANT TREES ARRIVE.

3. IF UNDISTURBED, A STABLE CLIMAX FOREST EMERGES.

Trees can be grouped based on their ability to adapt to different amounts of sunlight. Scientists call this adaptation tree tolerance. Pioneering plants are shade intolerant. That means these plants must have full sun to survive. In contrast, species that have the ability to grow in shade are called shade tolerant. Shade tolerant trees are adapted to low light and will grow in the shade of other trees. Most tree species fall between these two and are called mid-tolerant or intermediate in tolerance. Mid-tolerant trees, such as yellow birch, white ash, and red maple, are able to grow in partial shade. They take over the forest site from pioneer plants. After a period of time, their canopy closes over. Only those species that can grow in the densest shade, such as sugar maple and American beech, will survive. Seedlings of these shade tolerant species will grow slowly but continuously until openings in the canopy let more sunlight through and speed their growth. Tree tolerance explains changes that occur in a forest and why certain trees grow on different forest sites.

(TOP) **YELLOW BIRCH** *(BETULA ALLEGHANIENSIS)*

(BOTTOM) **SUGAR MAPLE** *(ACER SACCHARUM)*

Eventually, as the most tolerant species become dominant, they will perpetuate themselves in mature stands as part of a climax forest. Forest succession, going from shade intolerant pioneer plants to a tolerant climax forest, takes several hundred years.

## FORESTS OF THE ADIRONDACK REGION

The Adirondack region has five different types of forests. Often transitional forests, combining trees from two adjoining sites, separate the different forest types. The types of trees in each forest are determined by two environmental factors: elevation and soil composition. Starting in the lowest areas, white and red pine forests grow in soils filled with debris left from glaciers, where nutrients have been washed out of the soil. At slightly higher areas, there are wooded wetlands, or areas with poorly drained soil. Conifers such as red spruce and tamarack dominate these areas.

Flatlands and meadows have soil that is low in nutrients. This soil is made up of the sand and gravel deposited by glacial rivers. The mixed wood forests that grow in these areas include an assortment of conifers, along with intolerant deciduous trees such as paper birch, gray birch, fire cherry, and shadbush.

Above the flatlands, pure stands of deciduous trees grow on rich glacial till slopes with well-drained soil. At the highest elevations, the soil is thin and rocky. There, balsam fir and mountain paper birch, a pioneer species, dominate a mostly coniferous forest. Deciduous trees

**QUAKING ASPEN *(POPULUS TREMULOIDES)* (RIGHT SIDE OF PHOTO)**

may be found in mixed-wood forests, transition forests, and in pure stands.

Deciduous forests cover nearly 60 percent of all the land in the Adirondacks. These forests grow from the low slopes of the mountains to an altitude of 2,500 feet (760 m), where the soil is fertile (rich with nutrients) and well drained. Sugar maples and American beech dominate, but other deciduous species, including quaking aspen, paper birch, yellow birch, gray birch, black cherry, red maple, and white ash, also grow.

The deciduous forest is divided into layers. Each layer has its own characteristics and organisms, because each receives a different amount of sunlight and moisture. In spite of these differences, all layers are dependent on the others for the cycling of matter and the flow of energy.

The dominant trees of the deciduous ecosystem are broad-branching, with high-spreading crowns. The constant shade created by these trees is home for an understory (the layer between the canopy and the forest floor) of striped maple, a small tree rarely taller than 20 feet (6 m), and witchhobble, a shade-loving bush. The forest floor has various species of club mosses, as well as trilliums, wild sarsaparilla, and Solomon's seal.

Every year each tree produces huge quantities of leaves, wood, flowers, fruits, and seeds. All of these become food for insects and other animals of the forest. Birds such as redstarts, black-throated green warblers, and red-eyed vireos flit back and forth in the canopy. They gobble millions of mosquitoes, blackflies, and other forest insects. Squirrels scurry about and gather beechnuts and acorns for the coming winter. Red efts (a form of newt) hide under rocks and logs. Chipmunks, snowshoe hares, porcupines, deer, and black bears feed on the plants and leaf litter (the debris—dead leaves, branches, and seeds—dropped from trees and shrubs). Predators such as coyotes, foxes, and fishers eat the plant eaters.

In the soil layer, tiny protozoans, springtails, and mites, along with earthworms, millipedes, centipedes, and fungi, work at decomposing the leaf litter and carrion (remains of dead animals) left by other creatures.

Scientists estimate that as many as ten million leaves fall on each acre of forestland each year. Without decomposers, the forest would become buried under piles of dead leaves and animals. Decomposers make the nutrients from dead plants and animals available to living ones.

## STRUCTURE OF A FOREST

CANOPY

UNDERSTORY

FOREST FLOOR

# CHAPTER 2
# THE CANOPY

The uppermost layer of the deciduous forest is the canopy. In a climax forest, the canopy is made up of the leaves and branches of sugar maple and American beech trees. Their spreading branches block most of the sunlight from the forest floor. In younger forests, mid-tolerant trees, such as yellow birch, red maple, and white ash, might be growing in the canopy along with sugar maples and beech. Depending upon the age of the trees, the deciduous canopy ranges from 80 to 100 feet (24 to 30 m) above the ground. Old growth forests, with trees that are at least 150 years old, may have a canopy that is 100 feet (30 m) above the ground.

**DEPENDING UPON THE AGE OF THE TREES, THE DECIDUOUS CANOPY RANGES FROM 80 TO 100 FEET (24 TO 30 M) ABOVE THE GROUND.**

The leaves at the tops of these trees receive the most sunlight, so most of the canopy's photosynthesis is carried on there. The more leaves a tree has, the more sunlight it can absorb. Scientists estimate a full-grown maple tree may have one hundred thousand leaves. During photosynthesis, trees take in large amounts of carbon dioxide for producing food and release oxygen into the air.

The upper side of the canopy is not a good habitat for most animals. The sun's energy is too intense, and wind and rain can be violent. The canopy protects the rest of the forest. During the day, it shields the ground and keeps it from heating up too quickly. At night the canopy holds in heat and keeps the ground warm. Rain falls on the leafy roof and slowly trickles down to the ground. The canopy protects the soil beneath from washing away and shields the lower layers from high winds.

Thousands of insects live in the canopy just below the top surface. This is the zone of the leaf eaters—beetles, caterpillars, leafhoppers, aphids, and leaf mites—that thrive in this dense green world. The red-banded leafhopper sucks the sap from leaves. Leaf miners carve tunnels between the two surfaces of a leaf and eat the soft tissue inside. Spiders and insects that prey on others are abundant. Some insects spend their entire life cycle in the canopy.

This green world is also home to insect-eating birds that flit among the canopy's branches. One of the most common species is the red-eyed vireo. This bird is almost the same color as the leaves and is hard to see when it is perched on a branch high above. It reveals its presence with constant singing. A more colorful bird, the scarlet tanager, feeds heavily on caterpillars in the canopy.

(ABOVE) **RED-BANDED LEAFHOPPER**
*(GRAPHOCEPHELA COCCINEA)*
(RIGHT) **A RED-EYED VIREO** *(VIREO OLIVACEUS)*
**GUARDS ITS NEST.**

# PRIMARY PRODUCER: SUGAR MAPLE *(Acer saccharum)*

A sugar maple tree, ablaze with orange and red leaves, is a breathtaking autumn sight. Called the Queen of the Adirondacks, this tree, more than any other, symbolizes the deciduous forest.

Sugar maples can survive in a wide variety of soil types, but for maximum tree growth, the best soils are deep, moist, and well drained, with medium or fine textures. Such soils are common in glacial till areas of the Adirondacks.

The sugar maple can also grow under any canopy conditions. After a good seed year, the forest floor is a carpet of seedlings. The hardy seedlings grow, perhaps only 1 or 2 inches (2 to 5 cm) a year, until an opening in the canopy allows in more sunlight. Then they speed up their growth until they reach their full height and their crowns become part of the canopy.

For the first 30 to 40 years, sugar maples grow an average of 1 foot (0.3 m) in height and 0.2 inches (0.5 cm) in trunk diameter a year. Most sugar maples within a forest reach a height of 80 to 90 feet (24 to 27 m). Perhaps 30 feet (9 m) of this is clear trunk with a diameter of 2 to 3 feet (0.6 to 0.9 m). A few old-growth sugar maple trees in the Adirondacks are 300 to

400 years old with heights of up to 110 feet (34 m). After about 140 to 150 years, height growth stops and diameter growth slows. In open areas, where the tree doesn't have to compete with others for the sunlight, sugar maples are shorter and branch out lower down on the trunk.

Sugar maples have leaves with either three or five lobes arranged like the fingers on a hand. They are dark green on the top surface and paler underneath. Twigs are slender and shiny reddish brown. The bark is grayish and develops rough vertical ridges as the tree matures.

In early spring, the tree is covered with drooping clusters of greenish-yellow flowers that are pollinated by bees. Ten to twelve weeks later, double-winged seeds appear—small helicopters that float to the ground in August and September. Each fall, sugar maples produce a heavy leaf litter. The decaying leaves return many useful nutrients, such as calcium, potassium, phosphorus, and nitrogen, to the soil.

In spring, days become warmer, even though the ground may still be covered in snow. As the soil warms, the root hairs of the maple absorb water from melting snow and the thawed water in the ground. This intake of fluid forces sap up the tree. The sap brings sugars stored in the roots to the upper sections of the tree to nourish the slowly developing buds.

At night, chirps and squeaks high up in the trees announce the presence of southern flying squirrels. These squirrels don't really fly. They glide through the trees using fur-covered membranes that connect their front and hind legs. They resemble small parachutes as they swoop from upper branches to lower ones. These squirrels have been known to glide as far as 90 feet (nearly 27 m). Flying squirrels spend most of their time in the canopy, eating a variety of insects, bird eggs, and spiders.

The canopy changes from season to season. In spring, bare branches sprout buds, leaves, and then flowers. By summer the canopy is fully leafed out. Leaves serve as factories, producing food necessary for the tree's growth. Each leaf contains numerous chloroplasts, chlorophyll-containing cells in which photosynthesis takes place. These cells give the leaf its green color. There are also pigments of yellow, red, and orange in the leaf, but they are hidden by the green chlorophyll pigments. In autumn, changes in the length of daylight and changes in temperature cause chlorophyll production to slow. A layer of cells called the abscission layer begins to grow at the base of each leaf stem. This layer cuts off the tiny tubes that carry water and nutrients to the leaf. The leaf shuts down its production of food and slowly dies. The green chlorophyll in the leaf is used up and disappears. As the chlorophyll fades, red, yellow, or orange pigments become visible, and the leaf changes color. The abscission layer continues to grow across the stem until the leaf is barely attached. Rain or a gust of wind causes the leaf to fall. Once the leaf falls, the abscission cells act like corks for the tree, sealing in nutrients and water. These are stored in branches, trunk, and roots until the following spring. The tree will survive winter in a state of dormancy.

# CHAPTER 3
# THE UNDERSTORY AND MIDDLE LAYERS

Beneath the leaves of the highest trees is the shaded world of the understory. The understory contains younger trees of the dominant species. These smaller trees grow slowly and wait for an opening in the canopy to provide space and light. Other shade tolerant trees are also found at this level. One of these is the striped maple. This tree grows only in cool, moist spots. Striped maples do not tolerate direct sunlight and need only small bits of sunlight to flourish.

The understory contains all the trees' trunks. The trunks serve as

**BARK ON YOUNG TREES IS GENERALLY SMOOTH. AS TREES GROW, THE BARK SPLITS APART AND CRACKS. EACH KIND OF TREE HAS ITS OWN PATTERN OF ROUGH BARK.**

pipelines from the roots and soil. They carry water and nutrients to the leaves so that photosynthesis can occur. The trunk, the tree's stem, has five separate layers. From the outside to inner core they are outer bark, inner bark, cambium, sapwood, and heartwood. Each layer has a specific function.

The outer bark protects the tree from weather, disease, fire, insects, and animals. Bark on young trees is generally smooth. As trees grow, the bark splits apart and cracks. Each kind of tree has its own pattern of rough bark.

# PARTS OF A TREE

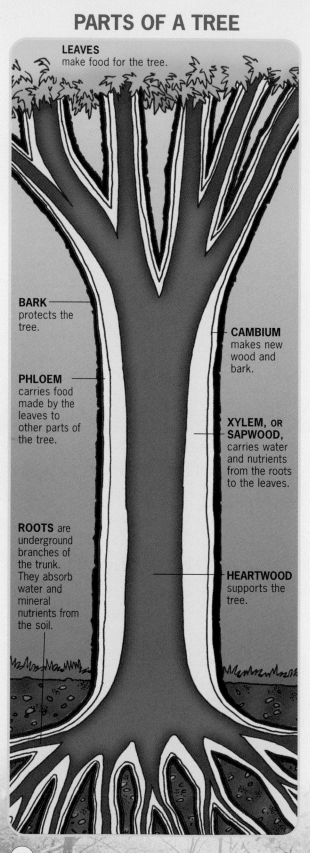

**LEAVES**
make food for the tree.

**BARK**
protects the tree.

**PHLOEM**
carries food made by the leaves to other parts of the tree.

**ROOTS** are underground branches of the trunk. They absorb water and mineral nutrients from the soil.

**CAMBIUM**
makes new wood and bark.

**XYLEM, OR SAPWOOD,**
carries water and nutrients from the roots to the leaves.

**HEARTWOOD**
supports the tree.

The inner bark, or phloem, contains tubelike cells through which food travels downward from the leaves and branches to all parts of the tree. The next layer, the cambium, produces new cells for the inner bark and for the sapwood. The xylem, or sapwood, carries water and nutrients up to the leaves and stores food for growth and seed production.

The innermost part of the trunk, the heartwood, gives the tree rigidity. The heartwood was once sapwood, but as the cells aged, they died. The heartwood is the oldest part of the tree.

Trees grow upward from the roots and upward and outward from the tips of the branches. The twigs have special cells on their ends that divide to make the twigs grow. Growth takes place in spring and summer when the leaves are actively involved in photosynthesis.

In a mature, climax forest, the area beneath the canopy is relatively empty except for the shade-loving plants that grow in dim light. When a forest has been disturbed by an ice storm, hurricane, or other severe weather, trees are sometimes blown over or lose large limbs. These openings in the canopy let sunlight shine into the understory. The extra sunlight provides energy to the plants that have been struggling in the shade. Soon the understory resembles a dense jungle with young trees, bushes, and vines.

The understory is habitat for many birds and insects. Every trunk is home to a vast number of microscopic worms and millions of insects. The pileated woodpecker, the largest woodpecker in the Adirondacks, hammers away at tree trunks searching for wood-boring beetles, carpenter ants, and other insects that live under the bark. This woodpecker makes its home in large holes in snags—dead, leafless trees that are still standing.

White-breasted nuthatches can be seen clinging upside down on tree trunks. By zigzagging down a tree headfirst, nuthatches find insects that woodpeckers miss. Beetles, insect eggs, caterpillars, and spiders, along with small seeds from evergreens, make up the nuthatches' diet. Often nuthatches store food for winter under pieces of bark.

Another bird that lives year-round in the understory is the tiny black-capped

(ABOVE) **PILEATED WOODPECKER**
(*DRYOCOPUS PILEATUS*)

(UPPER RIGHT) **WHITE-BREASTED NUTHATCH**
(*SITTA CAROLINESIS*)

(BOTTOM RIGHT) **BLACK-CAPPED CHICKADEE**
(*PARUS ATRICAPILLUS*)

chickadee, with its distinctive "chicka-dee-dee-dee" call. The chickadee, weighing no more than four pennies, makes its nest in a hole in a rotted tree branch high up in the understory.

Small brown bats sleep during the day wedged behind large chunks of loose bark on old trees. At night they wake up and fly out to consume large quantities of mosquitoes, flies, beetles, moths, and other flying insects.

The southern flying squirrel and many birds, such as the scarlet tanager, also build their nests in the understory, because it is relatively safe. The canopy above protects the smaller animals from being seen by hawks and owls. And they are high enough off the ground to escape ground predators.

## SHRUB LAYER

Shrubs are woody plants with several stems. They form a distinct layer no more than 6 or 7 feet (about 2 m) high in many forests. Their abundance or scarcity depends on how much sunlight reaches them.

Viburnum plants, such as hobblebush, often grow in maple and beech forests.

**RED-SHOULDERED HAWK**
*(BUTEO LINEATUS)*

**HOBBLEBUSH** *(VIBURNUM ALNIFOLIUM)*

# PRIMARY CONSUMER:
## EASTERN CHIPMUNK *(Tamias striatus)*

The eastern common chipmunk lives in all areas of the deciduous forest. This small mammal, between 8 and 10 inches (20 to 25 cm) long, is a member of the squirrel family. The chipmunk has a beautiful yellow- to chestnut-colored coat marked by five black stripes. Chin, throat, and underparts are white. Chipmunks live in a system of burrows beneath fallen logs or rocks, often with several entrances. They have different areas for eating and sleeping, and a nesting chamber where baby chipmunks are born.

Chipmunks usually choose to stay near the ground so they can reach their burrow quickly if danger threatens. But they are excellent climbers and will climb into the canopy to harvest beechnuts, their favorite food. Other staples of their diet are maple seeds, black cherries, nuts, fungi, and tubers, swollen underground stems that store nutrients needed for rapid plant growth in the spring. A chipmunk carries its food to its burrow in large cheek pouches.

Chipmunks are solitary, except during breeding season. The young are born thirty-one days after mating. They stay safe underground for more than one month. Soon after they emerge aboveground, the offspring leave to find their own burrows.

During the winter, chipmunks remain belowground. Their body temperature falls, and their body functions slow as they enter into a deep sleep. Every few days, they waken and eat some of their stored seeds, beechnuts, and dried berries. Nourished, the chipmunks go back to sleep. This winter adaptation is called torpor. The animals doze through the winter and venture aboveground again when the weather warms. Chipmunks can live for eight years, but few adults last longer than two to three years. They are an important food source for many predators, including the fisher—a member of the weasel family—and hawks, owls, coyotes, foxes, and bobcats.

Viburnums have pink and white flowers in spring. In autumn their leaves change to shades ranging from orange to a deep maroon. The twigs are a favorite browse (food) of deer.

Shrubs provide protective cover for many small animals, such as shrews, deer mice, and chipmunks. These animals make their burrows near bushes and forage in or under overhanging branches.

Many insects feed at the shrub level. Each spring, as the trees turn green, swarms of tiny blackflies hover in the shrubs. They are part of a group of insects that are called buffalo gnats because they have humped backs that resemble the American bison, or buffalo. In the Adirondacks, more than one dozen species of blackflies feed on the warm-blooded animals living at ground level. Once a female blackfly has mated, she looks for a meal of blood. She needs certain animal proteins contained in blood for proper egg development. The yearly explosion of blackflies provides an important food source for the many birds that need extra protein in preparation for laying eggs and feeding chicks.

Two birds that nest beneath the branches in the shrub layer are the ovenbird and the rose-breasted grosbeak. The ovenbird got its name because it builds its nest on the ground in a mound of leaves and grasses, and the nest resembles the earthen oven that early settlers used. The ovenbird's call sounds like "teacher-teacher-teacher." Rose-breasted grosbeaks

(ABOVE) **AN OVENBIRD (SEIURUS AUROCAPILLUS) FEEDS ITS YOUNG.**

(RIGHT) **A BLACKFLY (SIMULIIDAE) BITES A HUMAN HAND.**

have mostly black feathers on their backs and wings and a white lower body. Their breast feathers are pinkish red. These birds build their nests in shrubs 5 to 20 feet (1.5 to 6 m) from the ground. The male shares egg incubation duty with the female. Although they nest in the shrub layer of the deciduous forest, rose-breasted grosbeaks feed in nearby fields, where they devour huge numbers of june bugs and potato beetles.

Spring peepers and other tree frogs also live on the branches and shrubs of this layer. Tree frogs are tiny, averaging 1 inch (3 cm) or less in length. In early spring thousands of male spring peepers produce a daily chorus that starts in late afternoon and continues throughout the evening. The daily mating call of male tree frogs may run from late April until mid-June.

In July the places where sunlight reaches the ground are often covered with huckleberries, raspberries, and blackberries, which grow on brierlike shrubs. Blueberries, able to tolerate poor soil conditions, often grow in dense, shrubby clumps. Black bears, raccoons, and blue jays are frequent visitors to the berry patches.

**BLACK BEARS (URSUS AMERICANUS)**

**BLACKBERRIES (RUBUS)**

# CHAPTER 4
# THE GROUND LAYER AND SOIL

The floor of the deciduous forest consists of the ground layer and the soil. The forest floor is covered with what some refer to as the herb layer. Herbs are seed-producing plants with soft stems, rather than woody ones. This layer is made up of wildflowers, grasses, ferns, mosses, lichens, and fungi that grow close to the ground.

Seed-bearing plants in the ground layer most often grow in the early spring. These plants rush to sprout, produce leaves, and bloom before the canopy fills with leaves. As the trees' leaves fill out, less sunlight reaches the ground, and the flowers die back to the soil, though the roots live on. These early spring flowers are called ephemerals. They bloom for less than two weeks.

In May two of the first plants to appear are the spring beauty and the trout lily, also known as adder's-tongue. The trout lily bears a small, single yellow flower on a stalk. Mice and voles eat the trout lily's tubers. Deer nibble on the leaves.

Another spring flower, the purple trillium, also known as stinkpot, has an odor like decaying flesh that attracts pollinating insects to its dull reddish

**WHITE-FOOTED MOUSE (PEROMYSCUS LEUCOPUS)**

flower. Large patches of bloodroot also bloom in spring. Bloodroot was named for a reddish-orange liquid that is found in its stems and roots. Blue (really purplish) and white violets, jack-in-the-pulpits, and miterwort are some of the other plants that are adapted to the short spring growing season.

## SPORE-BEARING PLANTS

Mosses, liverworts, lichens, and ferns are plants that reproduce from spores instead of seeds. Spores are tiny one-celled reproductive bodies that are released into the air like microscopic particles of dust.

Mosses reproduce themselves by a method called alternation of generation. One generation of the moss plant forms spores. If a spore lands in a place with sufficient moisture and warmth, it begins to grow. The single cell divides into many new cells. These branch out in many directions and spread over the ground. Soon buds appear and develop into the new generation of plants.

The next generation forms gametes, male and female reproductive cells. When the plant is wet with rain or dew, sperm cells can swim to unite with the egg cells, and fertilization takes place. A new plant grows from each union. This new generation produces spore capsules, and the process begins again.

Liverworts reproduce in much the same way as mosses. The *Marchantia* liverwort has spore capsules with coiled threads that act like springs. When the capsules split open, the threads uncoil and shoot out the spores.

**BLOODROOT (*SANGUINARIA CANADENSIS*)**

Mosses and liverworts usually grow less than 1 inch (3 cm) tall because they lack xylem and phloem, the interior tubes found in trees and flowering plants that transport food and water. Mosses and liverworts grow well in the moist environment of the deciduous forest because they can absorb water and nutrients directly from the air into their leaves and stems. These plants are often pioneer plants, growing in areas of the forest that have been disturbed. Cord moss and *Marchantia* liverwort are often the first plants to appear after a forest fire.

Mosses have variable shapes, with branched stems and green leaves that are only one cell thick. The leaves vary in color depending on whether they are moist or dry. Club mosses are related to ferns and look like miniature fir trees. Club mosses produce spores upon tiny stalks that look like clubs.

Mosses, liverworts, and lichens do not have roots. Instead these plants have rootlike threads called rhizoids that attach to tree trunks, branches, dead tree stumps, and even rocks. Rhizoids serve as natural sponges that soak up moisture and release it slowly. They also help to keep soil from washing away during rains.

Liverworts grow flat on the ground in branching ribbon shapes. Recently scientists have uncovered evidence that suggests that liverworts were the first plants to grow on land. Of all known plants, the liverworts' genetic makeup is closest to that of the green algae (microscopic plants) that live in water.

Lichens are really two organisms joined together, a fungus and a

**MOSSES, LIVERWORTS, AND LICHENS DO NOT HAVE ROOTS. INSTEAD THESE PLANTS HAVE ROOTLIKE THREADS CALLED RHIZOIDS THAT ATTACH TO TREE TRUNKS, BRANCHES, DEAD TREE STUMPS, AND EVEN ROCKS.**

blue-green alga. The fungus provides water and minerals to the alga. The alga, which contains chlorophyll, lives protected among fungal threads and produces food for itself and for the fungus. Lichens grow as a crust, a leafy flap, or a beardlike tuft on bare rock, soil, dead wood, animal bones, or living bark. Lichens secrete acids that can break down rock into soil. They grow very slowly, often less than 0.5 inch (1.3 cm) per year.

Ferns are among the oldest plants on earth to have true stems, roots, and leaves. The stems, called rhizomes, grow underground and have xylem and phloem tubes that carry water and food to the fronds, or leaves. Roots sprout from the underground stems and spread out to anchor the plant. The deciduous forest's ferns are hardy plants with tough, leathery fronds. Some of the most common varieties are the polypody fern (which can grow on trunks of trees or on the ground), the bracken fern, the male fern, the autumn fern, and the giant wood fern.

Like mosses, ferns have two stages in their life cycle. The fern plant is the sporophyte stage, the stage that produces spores. Tiny spore cases, each containing dozens of spores, develop on the underside of the fronds. When the spores are mature, they are released from the spore cases. Spores that are fortunate enough to land in a damp spot germinate and grow into small heart-shaped plants called prothallia. This is the gametophyte stage, the stage that produces gametes, or sex cells. The prothallium, which is less than 0.25 inch (0.6 cm) tall, produces both male and female sex cells. When ripe, the male cells

**LICHENS (EUMYCOTA) COVER THIS FALLEN LOG.**

**BRACKEN FERN (*PTERIDIUM AQUILINUM*)**

swim toward the female cells in a thin film of water from dew or rain. Fertilization takes place, and new fern plants grow. The prothallium, no longer needed, dies.

Most ferns are perennial, living for several years. Each autumn the fronds die, but they do not fall off the plant. Instead the dead fronds cover the base of the plant, insulating the underground parts during the winter.

## FUNGI

Mushrooms also grow in the herb layer. They are the fruiting bodies of fungi. Fungi are not part of either the plant or the animal kingdom but are in their own kingdom. Scientists estimate that more than sixty-five thousand species exist, and new ones are discovered each year. Molds and yeasts are also types of fungi.

Fungi reproduce by spores. Each spore is capable of growing into a new fungus if it lands in a suitable place. A thread called a hypha grows from the spore and divides in two. It keeps dividing until there are hundreds of hyphae. These threads form a web called a mycelium. A fruiting body grows from the mycelium and produces more spores. Fungi do not contain chlorophyll, so they are unable to make their own food. They feed on living or dead animals and plants and grow in soil or on leaves, moss, logs, stumps, or standing trees.

Most fungi produce their spores in mushrooms, which are umbrella-shaped fruiting bodies. Under the mushroom's cap hang thin folds of tissue called gills. Spores are produced on the surface of the gills. A common mushroom can produce five hundred thousand spores. When the spores are ripe, they drop from the mushroom. Most fungus spores are spread by the wind. Some glide away in rain or other moisture. Many of the shelflike bracket fungi shed their spores only during wet weather.

Other spores are carried away by animals. The stinkhorn fungus, named because it has an odor of rotting meat, is covered with an olive-green slime that contains spores. Flies, attracted by the smell, feed on the slime and carry away the spores.

Most fungi have a fruiting season that lasts only a few days. Some, like the shaggymane, have a split season. They grow in the spring and then again in the fall. The ganoderma fungus sheds its spores continuously, night and day, for five or six months of the year. Fungi grow best in moist areas, and great numbers of fruiting bodies appear after rain.

Thousands of species of fungi are found in the moist deciduous forest. Some common species are the giant puffball, which releases spores in a great cloud; the horn of plenty, found in leaf litter; the shaggymane, with edges that decay into an inky mass; the turkey tail; the jack o'lantern; and the long-stemmed oyster fungus.

## HOW DO FUNGI FEED?

The hyphae of fungi produce a chemical that oozes out into the host plant or animal. The chemical breaks the host down into simpler substances. Fungi then

(ABOVE) **SHAGGY MANE MUSHROOM**
**(COPRINUS COMATUS)**

(TOP LEFT) **JACK O'LANTERN MUSHROOM**
**(OMPHALOTUS ILLUDENS)**

(BOTTOM LEFT) **TURKEY TAIL FUNGI**
**(TRAMETES VERSICOLOR)**

absorb water, minerals, sugar, and starch through the thin walls of their hyphae.

Fungi are either saprophytes, which feed on dead plants and animals, or parasites, which feed on living things. Saprophytes help clear away dead plants and animals that would otherwise pile up in the forest. Most parasitic fungi cause harm to the plant or animal by spreading their hyphae among the host's cells and secreting chemicals that break down living tissues. Often these fungi kill the host plant or animal.

One species of bracket fungus that grows on the trunks of birch trees is an example of a parasitic fungus. The fungus looks like a small shelf sticking out from the trunk. After being attacked by this fungus, birch trees seldom live longer than forty years. Other examples of parasitic fungi found on plants are white powdery mildew and reddish-brown rust. They produce spores in little capsules at the end of microscopic hyphae. These parasites feed on leaves, causing them to lose water and eventually wilt and die.

Some fungi live in a close relationship with plants but do not harm them. This kind of mutually beneficial relationship is called symbiosis. The mycelium of certain kinds of fungi, called mycorrhizal fungi, covers and sometimes penetrates the roots of certain trees. This partnership is a symbiotic relationship. The fungus absorbs vitamins, simple proteins, and sugars from the tree. In return, the fungus provides the tree's root hairs with certain minerals, such as phosphate, nitrate, and potassium, that are essential for the tree's growth.

Fungi continue to grow in the same place until the nutrients they require for growth have been exhausted. The fruiting bodies of fungi are food for many animals such as mice, voles, and rabbits. Even if the fruiting body is eaten, the mycelium continues to grow on its host.

## AT GROUND LEVEL

Rotting logs, tree stumps, and fallen branches on the ground layer are often covered by mosses and other plants. This woody debris provides food and homes for many animals.

# DECOMPOSER: GIANT POLYPORE BRACKET FUNGUS (*Meripilus giganteus*)

Bracket fungi are also called shelf fungi, because their fruiting bodies, called basidiocarps, extend out horizontally from trees, like small shelves. The basidiocarps are woody or leathery, never soft like mushroom caps. As many as one thousand different species of bracket fungi exist. Most are found in woodland areas, where they cause rapid decay of tree stumps and fallen trees. A few members of the family feed on decaying matter in the soil.

Unlike many mushrooms, which shrivel and die after a few days, bracket fungus basidiocarps may last for several months. The mycelium that produces the bracket lives in the tissues of the tree and produces spores for several years. Eventually the fungus kills the tree, but it will continue living on the snag or stump until no wood pulp is left.

One bracket fungus that is often seen in the deciduous forest in autumn is *Meripilus giganteus*, the giant polypore. This fungus produces large masses of rounded, wavy-edged, soft plates on the trunk and the roots of beech trees. The upper surface of the fungus is brownish yellow to chestnut-brown when fresh, and the lower surface is creamy white. With age the color darkens and the fruiting body deteriorates into a black, slimy mess.

*Meripilus giganteus* often attacks the roots of beech trees. Months later the tree will fall over or will be blown over in a windstorm. The exposed roots of such a tree have most of the woody tissue eaten away.

Black bears make their dens in hollow trees or sleep on the ground under brush piles or dense shrubs. Bears are omnivores, eating both plants and animals. They forage for food on the ground level, eating whatever plant or animal matter is most available. Their diet consists of plants, berries, seeds, insects, carrion, small mammals, reptiles, and amphibians. With strong front claws, bears can tear open rotten logs in search of insect grubs and other larvae (immature insects).

The ground level contains a variety of insects, such as crickets, as well as slugs, centipedes, and millipedes. Many species of ants nest under logs and in tree stumps. These ground-dwelling creatures are part of the diet of small mammals, such as shrews and mice. Shrews resemble small mice with long noses. They live under leaf litter and rely on their sense of touch to find their prey.

Many kinds of amphibians, such as salamanders, newts, and wood frogs, live among the leaves on the ground. A large chickenlike bird, the ruffed grouse, makes its nest on the forest floor, usually in dense underbrush. Males make a drumming

(TOP) **SLUG (STYLOMMATOPHORA)**
(BOTTOM) **CRICKET (GRYLLINAE)**

**RUFFED GROUSE (BONASA UMBELLUS)**

noise by beating their short, powerful wings inward toward their inflated chests. The grouse repeats the drumming over and over to attract females and to keep other males away from his territory. This bird, sometimes called a partridge, is vulnerable to ground predators such as foxes, coyotes, bobcats, and fishers.

## SOIL

The soil is made up of four primary components: mineral particles, decayed organic matter, live organisms, and space for air and water. Leaf litter (leaf parts and whole leaves), logs, branches, seeds, and dead animals are part of the top layer of soil. Bacteria and fungi digest this top layer of litter, causing it to break down and decay. Leaves decay at different rates. Maple leaves rot quickly. Beech leaves decompose more slowly, and it may take bacteria and fungi two or three years to break down oak leaves. On average, most kinds of deciduous leaves decompose within one year.

Underneath this top layer there is a crumbly layer called humus. The humus layer provides nutrients for the roots of trees and other plants. Humus is a deep layer of decomposed leaves and other organic material that has been thoroughly mixed and broken down by earthworms, insects, fungi, and bacteria. Millions of protozoa (tiny one-celled animals), springtails, mites, earthworms, fly larvae, wood lice, bacteria, and fungi live in this layer. This area is a tangle of crisscrossed roots and thin, living threads of fungus hyphae. Scientists estimate there could be as many as one hundred thousand box mites in

FISHER (MARTES PENNANTI)

1 cubic yard (0.8 cubic m) of leaf litter, and 10,000 pounds (4,500 kilograms) of living organisms in 1 acre (0.4 hectare) of soil.

Organisms receive nutrients in the humus layer of soil. The transfer takes place in pore spaces, the spaces that contain air and water in between the mineral and nutrient particles. Growing conditions are ideal when pore spaces contain equal parts of air and water. This allows for root expansion, transfer of nutrients from the soil to living organisms, and movement of organisms through the soil.

Under the humus layer are layers of silt, sand, clay, and rocks in the process of being broken down into soil particles. These particles will nourish the forest in the years to come.

Each spring the yearly cycle of growth begins when the ground warms and the ice in the soil melts. Millions of tiny root hairs grow out from plant roots and absorb water and nutrients. Root hairs live for just a few months. They are continually replaced by new ones until autumn. Then photosynthesis shuts down.

Roots grow outward and into the soil, creating an anchoring framework. A tree 80 feet (24 m) high may have roots only 6 to 8 feet (about 2 m) deep. But those roots may spread 80 feet (24 m) from the tree in all directions. As roots age, they no longer transport water and nutrients, but they continue to be part of the anchoring system of the tree.

**WHITE TRILLIUM (TRILLIUM GRANDIFLORUM) GROWS WELL AMONG THE ROOTS OF AN AMERICAN BEECH (FAGUS GRANDIFOLIA).**

# CHAPTER 5
# BIODIVERSITY WITHIN THE DECIDUOUS FOREST

Old-growth forests are forests with trees that have lived for three hundred years or longer. In addition to the age of the trees, scientists characterize an old-growth forest as having a well-developed canopy with a significant number of snags, downed trees, and woody debris, and with an understory of small trees, shrubs, herbs, ferns, mosses, and lichens. All these characteristics indicate a rich biodiversity of plants and wildlife.

All of the layers of the forest work together in a balanced partnership among plants, animals, and habitat.

ALL OF THE LAYERS OF THE FOREST WORK TOGETHER IN A BALANCED PARTNERSHIP AMONG PLANTS, ANIMALS, AND HABITAT. GENERALLY, THE GREATER THE BIODIVERSITY OF AN ECOSYSTEM, THE HEALTHIER AND MORE STABLE IT IS.

Generally, the greater the biodiversity of an ecosystem, the healthier and more stable it is.

Each layer of the forest is dependent upon each other layer. The canopy produces food from the sun's energy, which enables the trees and thousands of insects, birds, and other animals to live. It also protects the other layers from heavy winds and driving rain, and provides warmth, moisture, and increased humidity. The trunks in the understory transport water and nutrients. Shrubs and other middle-layer plants help prevent erosion by putting down roots that hold the soil. Birds, insects, mammals, and other wildlife use the canopy, understory, and ground layers for food and shelter. Fungi, earthworms, bacteria, and the other decomposers in the soil play a vital role in breaking down the leaf litter and dead animals so that nutrients are returned to the soil to be used by the plants and animals of the forest.

The diversity of life in the Adirondacks is demonstrated by the fact that the area is home to approximately sixty-two species of trees, fifty-four species of mammals, and more than two hundred species of birds. Scientists are surveying the number of species of reptiles and amphibians. The total number of fungi and invertebrates, or animals without backbones, may never be known. But what ecologists do know for certain is that all of these species are interdependent and work in balance.

For example, the trout lily, an early ephemeral plant, absorbs potassium and nitrogen from water during snowmelt, while other plants are still dormant. Later during the summer, these nutrients are available to other plants when the aboveground parts of the lily die and decompose.

Another early bloomer, squirrel corn, has an appendage called an aril on each seed. The arils attract ants. They drag the seeds to their nests to eat the arils. The seeds scattered by ants spread the squirrel corn to other areas of the forest. The black cherry tree depends on birds to spread its seeds. Birds eat the fruit of black cherry trees, and the seeds are scattered in their droppings.

Under the ground, burrowing earthworms pull down leaves from the litter for their food. Nutrients are returned to the soil after earthworms and other decomposers eat the leaves. Earthworm burrows let air into the soil and allow rainwater to seep down to tiny root hairs.

Fungi are also connected to processes in all parts of the forest. Flies and beetles lay their eggs inside fungi. When the grubs hatch they have a ready food supply. Ambrosia beetles allow fungus hyphae to grow in their tunnels. The beetles eat the fruiting bodies of the fungi and the fungi feed on beetle droppings.

(ABOVE) **SQUIRREL CORN**
*(DICENTRA CANADENSIS)*

(TOP LEFT) **TROUT LILY**
*(ERYTHRONIUM AMERICANUM)*

(BOTTOM LEFT) **EARTHWORM**
**(LUMBRICIDAE)**

**A SAW-WHET OWL** (*AEGOLIUS ACADICUS*)
**NESTS IN A HOLLOW TREE TRUNK.**

Heart rot fungi decay the already dead heartwood in the center of living trees, producing hollow cavities. These cavities provide nest holes for owls, wood ducks, and other birds; roosts for bats; and homes for a great variety of invertebrates.

Many trees have a symbiotic relationship with fungi. Some species of fungi store phosphate, a mineral essential for a tree's growth, and gradually release it to the tree. Scientists have found that deciduous trees such as larch, oak, beech, and birch benefit from this mycorrhizal relationship with fungi.

Insects and other invertebrates are a large part of the forest's biodiversity. A rotting log on the forest floor can support up to seventeen hundred different species of insects and other invertebrates. Researchers have also calculated that more than three hundred species of insects may live on one mature oak tree.

Beavers, the largest rodents in North America, are found throughout the ecosystem. Hardwood bark is a large part of their diet. Ponds and wet meadows created by beaver dams support more than one hundred bird species and twenty other animal species.

Predators like the eastern coyote help keep the ecosystem balanced. Without coyotes and other large predators who kill deer, the deer population would increase substantially. Heavy deer browsing could result in the shrub and ground layer of the forest being destroyed, leaving only bare dirt. Spring flowers, bushes, and shrubs would be gone, along with the animals that feed and live in the shrub layer.

The eastern coyote is a also a boon to ravens, martens, fishers, and foxes. They scavenge carrion that the coyote has abandoned.

Any change that affects one species can have a significant effect on other plants and animals. In the early part of the twentieth century, the chestnut blight killed most of the American chestnut trees in the Adirondacks. This meant the loss of chestnuts, a major source of food for chipmunks, deer, and bears. Five species of insects that depended on chestnut trees have also disappeared.

AMERICAN BEAVER *(CASTOR CANADENSIS)*

# SECONDARY CONSUMER:
## EASTERN COYOTE *(Canis latrans)*

The intelligent eastern coyote is a relative newcomer to the Adirondacks. It arrived from Canada in the 1920s and has become fully established throughout the area. Researchers believe the eastern coyote interbred with the timber wolf. That explains why the eastern coyote is larger than its western cousin. Many wildlife geneticists, or scientists who study inherited traits, believe the eastern coyote is a species in the process of evolution: it is a hybrid, part wolf and part coyote, and in time may become a separate species. The male weighs from 20 to 50 pounds (9 to 23 kilograms) and has an overall length of 4 to 5 feet (1.2 to 1.5 m). The coyote's light brown fur is long and soft, well suited to protect it from the cold.

The coyote is best known for its yelping, howling cry. The howling seems to be a means of communication. It usually brings a reply, which is followed by another prolonged cry and finally a volley of raucous yelping from several other individuals.

The animal's keen senses of hearing, smell, and vision make it an amazing predator. It can smell food more than 1 mile (more than 1.6 km) away. Coyotes run at an average speed of 25 miles (40 km) per hour, but they can reach speeds of 40 miles (64 km) per hour in short bursts. Individuals often hunt small prey alone, but hunt large prey and defend large carcasses in groups.

Coyotes den in hollow logs, under fallen trees, or in

underground burrows. The same shelter may be used for several years in a row. Mating takes place in February or March, and babies are born about two months later. On average, a litter consists of six pups covered with fine brown hair. The father brings food to the den until the pups are old enough to hunt on their own.

Coyotes are primarily flesh eaters. Rabbits, hares, and small rodents are staples of their diet. In the winter, adult deer account for much of the coyotes' food. Deer can't run in heavy snow, so they "yard up," or gather together in open areas. A group of deer in the open is easy hunting for coyotes.

# CHAPTER 6
# PEOPLE AND THE ADIRONDACK FOREST

Prehistoric people first lived in the area of Lake Champlain ten thousand years ago, after the glacial ice melted. Later, Native Americans of the Algonquin language groups hunted, fished, and collected plant foods from the lakeshores and river valleys of the region.

Still later, another group of people, the Iroquois, farmed in the Mohawk and St. Lawrence River valleys. The rich plant and animal life of the Adirondacks was essential to the Iroquois way of life. Some historians believe that the name "Adirondack" may have been derived from the Iroquois word *ha-de-ron-dah,* which means "bark eater," a mocking name the Iroquois gave to the Algonquins.

French explorers Samuel de Champlain and Father Isaac Jogues, a missionary, were the first Europeans to visit the region. They arrived in the early seventeenth century. Both France and England claimed ownership of the area. By the eighteenth century, scattered French and British settlements and military posts were located along Lake George and Lake Champlain. The French

**THE ALGONQUIN PEOPLE BUILT HOMES IN THE ADIRONDACKS.**

and Indian War (1754–1763) settled the claims of England and France in favor of the British.

During the Revolutionary War (1775–1783), the Colonists captured Fort Ticonderoga, along the eastern border of the Adirondacks. Several battles with the British occurred in the area. Except for these eastern fringes of the forest, the Adirondacks remained unexplored.

This changed as the United States became more industrialized. The discovery of iron ore in the Adirondacks fueled efforts to develop iron mining, furnaces, and forges. At the same time, logging began in earnest. Rivers flowing out from the center of the Adirondack region were used to transport millions of pine and spruce logs to sawmills around the base of the mountains. Paper mills consumed thousands of spruce and fir trees. Timber was used to construct buildings, furniture, ships, and fuel. Factories burned wood to produce steam for their engines. One salt manufacturer in Syracuse, New York, burned two hundred thousand cords of wood each year. A cord is a stack of wood that measures 4 feet (1.2 m) high, 4 feet deep, and 8 feet (2.4 m) long. Other factories burned wood to produce charcoal, a fuel used in the iron and steel industries. To keep up with the demand for wood, New York State had seven thousand sawmills in 1845. New York led the country in production of lumber. Bark stripped from hemlock trees fed the state's first leather tanning factories. Soon there were fifteen hundred factories for extracting tannin from tree bark.

TO KEEP UP WITH THE DEMAND FOR WOOD, NEW YORK STATE HAD SEVEN THOUSAND SAWMILLS IN 1845. NEW YORK LED THE COUNTRY IN PRODUCTION OF LUMBER.

Destruction of woodlands resulted in topsoil erosion and periods of flooding. As vast areas of forest were cleared by loggers, wildlife habitats were completely destroyed. Bounty hunters killed off the gray wolf, the mountain lion, and the wolverine. Unregulated hunting took its toll on other animals, such as white-tailed deer, beavers, wild turkeys, and passenger pigeons. The passenger pigeon, a wild pigeon about 15 inches (38 cm) long, was found in large numbers all over the Adirondacks. Each day during the nesting season, thousands of birds were shot and shipped to New York City. They sold for one to two cents each. Eventually the hunters killed them all. The last passenger pigeon died in a zoo in 1914.

In 1869 William H. H. Murray wrote *Adventures in the Wilderness.* The book was a kind of travel guide that praised the natural beauty of the Adirondacks. It gave routes and costs, and advice on clothes to wear, lists of sporting equipment needed, and even how to deal with blackflies. The public bought thousands of copies. The railroad offered a copy of this book free with every purchase of a round-trip ticket to the Adirondacks.

As a result, the region became a popular vacation destination. Fresh mountain air was thought to be a cure for tuberculosis, so people came for their health as well. Hotels sprang up, with guides to serve visitors to the area. Wealthy families built elaborate estate houses they called "camps" and "camped out" during the summer months. The wilderness was becoming less wild.

Politicians and journalists condemned the destruction of the forests, but the lumbering and mining continued. In 1872 Verplanck Colvin was hired to supervise yearly topographical surveys of the Adirondack region. Colvin, along with two other preservation advocates, Charles Sprague Sargent and Franklin B. Hough, "the father of American Forestry," decried the abuse of the forests. They wanted the region to become a vast public park.

In his annual reports to the legislature, Colvin called for the creation of an Adirondack Forest Preserve. In 1874 his report stated, "Unless the region be preserved essentially in its present wilderness condition, the ruthless burning and destruction of the forest will slowly, year after year, creep onward . . . and vast areas of naked rock, arid sand and gravel will alone remain to receive the bounty of the clouds unable to retain it." Persuaded by such testimony, the state legislature established the Adirondacks Forest Preserve in 1885 and later the Adirondack Park in 1892. In 1894 New Yorkers voted to add to the state constitution that the forest preserve shall be "forever kept as wild forest lands."

Much of the Adirondack forest looks as it did three hundred years ago. Most of the trees are part of second-growth forests, those that have regrown on land that was once cleared. These trees are less than one hundred years old. About 203,000 acres (82,000 hectares) of original old growth forest can still be found there.

## PESTS AND DISEASES

In spite of conservation efforts to keep the area as "wild forest lands," the impact of people in the nineteenth and twentieth centuries can not be dismissed. Along with human visitors came two deadly pests: the chestnut blight fungus and the gypsy moth.

During colonial times, American chestnut trees made up as much as 25 percent of the deciduous forest. This tree was a source of nuts and high-grade lumber until the turn of the century, when the chestnut blight fungus arrived. The fungus was brought to the United States in 1900 from the Far East, perhaps on imported lumber. Within a few years, American chestnut trees began to die. By the 1930s, the blight had killed almost every mature chestnut tree in America.

A naturalist brought gypsy moth caterpillars from Europe. He wanted to cross the gypsy moth with the silkworm moth to produce hardier silkworms. Unfortunately some of his gypsy moths escaped. Gypsy moth caterpillars are voracious eaters. They can completely defoliate a tree, devouring up to 50 square inches (320 square cm) of leaves in less than two months. Foresters spend thousands of dollars every year trying to control this pest.

Other tree pests that harm the forest are beech scale insects and Dutch elm disease, both introduced from Europe. Dutch elm disease, spread by elm bark beetles, has destroyed most of the elm trees in this country.

In spite of harmful insects, blights, and natural disasters, humans are responsible for most of the destruction that has taken place in the Adirondacks. Current major problems, created and made worse by human activity, include:

clear-cutting of the forest, global warming, and acid rain.

## CLEAR-CUTTING

Some loggers use the clear-cutting method of lumbering. They cut down every tree with a diameter larger than 2 inches (5 cm). The destruction of plant and animal life in clear-cut areas alters the ecosystem for generations. Without tree roots and shrubs to hold down the soil, rain and the meltwater from snow erode the land, destroy valuable topsoil, and cause mud slides that clog and damage rivers and streams. When a clear-cut area is restored by a lumber company, often only one or a few species are planted. Thus the biodiversity of plants and animals in the natural forest is lost.

The Department of Environmental Conservation of New York State works with the lumber industry and

**GYPSY MOTH *(PORTHETRIA DISPAR)* LARVA**

private landowners to better manage the forest and use more environmentally sound methods for the logging and harvesting of trees. They encourage owners to adopt a sustained yield approach. That way portions of the forest are harvested at regular intervals, with enough time between harvests to allow the forest to recover.

Two recommended methods of lumbering are called shelterwood cutting and seed-tree cutting. Shelterwood cutting involves cutting down only a portion of the trees in a forest, so a partial canopy cover remains until new trees become established. Seed-tree cutting involves leaving several large trees on a site to provide a seed source to renew the forest. These forest management strategies minimize the disturbance created by lumbering. There is little damage to soil, water, or wildlife. Many species of wildlife need the young, dense vegetation that quickly grows on cut-over forested sites. Pioneer species soon move into the cut areas, increasing their biodiversity. As a result of good

forest management, the number of big trees—those having a diameter of 19 inches (48 cm) or larger—has increased by 33 percent since 1980.

## GLOBAL WARMING

Widespread clear-cutting, as practiced in the last century, increases the problem of global warming, or the greenhouse effect. The earth's atmosphere contains several gases, such as carbon dioxide and methane, that are known as greenhouse gases. Like the glass of a greenhouse, these gases trap the sun's rays as they are reflected from the earth's surface, preventing them from escaping into space. This warms the planet. Without the greenhouse effect, the earth would be too cold for life as we know it.

Burning fossil fuels, such as coal, oil, and gasoline, releases carbon dioxide into the air. Too much carbon dioxide in the atmosphere traps too much heat. This causes the average temperature of the earth to rise. This is called global warming. These warmer temperatures could cause melting of the polar ice caps. This would raise sea levels, flooding coastal cities like New York City, Boston, and San Francisco. Some fear that as the planet warms, many plants and animals, unable to adapt to the warmer temperatures, would eventually become extinct. Cold-weather species such as the sugar maple might die off.

Trees are the earth's primary regulators of carbon dioxide. A full-grown tree consumes 13 pounds (6 kilograms) of carbon dioxide every year during photosynthesis. But human activity releases more carbon dioxide into the atmosphere than is being consumed by the existing trees. The problem is made worse by deforestation and clear-cutting. The fewer trees consume even less carbon dioxide. Solutions to curb global warming include reducing emissions from the burning of fossil fuels, promoting good forest management, planting more trees, and conserving existing old growth forests.

## ACID RAIN

Acid rain threatens the deciduous forests. Acid rain is formed when two gases, sulfur dioxide and nitrogen oxide, are released into the atmosphere. These two gases are by-products of the burning of coal, oil, and natural gas by factories, power stations, and automobiles. The gases mix with water in the atmosphere. Sulfur dioxide becomes sulfuric acid, and nitrogen oxide becomes nitric acid. These acids fall to earth as tiny droplets that are generally referred to as acid rain. "Acid precipitation" is a more accurate name for the problem, because the acid is found in snow, sleet, fog, and clouds, as well as rain.

The acid level of soil or water is measured in units on the pH scale. The scale ranges from 0 to 14. A solution with a pH of 7 is neutral. A reading below 7 means the solution is acid. Pure water measures 7.0. Normal rainwater measures about 5.6, which is slightly acid because carbon dioxide from the atmosphere dissolves into the water that makes up clouds. Acid rain is far more acidic than normal rain. Its acidity is closer to that of vinegar, which has a pH of 3.0, or lemon juice, which has a pH of 2.5.

Sulfur and nitrogen from acid rain accumulate in the soil until it rains again, and then they are turned into sulfuric acid

and nitric acid in the groundwater. Excess acid left in the soil by acid precipitation leaches out important nutrients. Leaching means that chemicals dissolve and drain away. Acid rain leaches minerals such as calcium and magnesium from the soil. Calcium is essential for wood formation in trees; when this mineral is missing, growth slows. Lack of essential minerals weakens trees. They become susceptible to changes in climate, more vulnerable to disease, and subject to defoliation from insects. Acid rain kills trees by reducing their ability to deal with stress. If there is sufficient calcium and magnesium available, trees can survive such challenges.

The Adirondacks have suffered some of the worst acid rain damage in the nation. Many coal-burning utility plants are in the Ohio River Valley of the Midwest. The prevailing winds blow the pollutants to the northeast, where the Adirondack Mountains intercept the pollutant-filled rain clouds. Day after day, pollution drips from the trees.

Spotted or mottled leaves are a warning sign of acid rain damage. Trees affected by acid rain generally die from the top down. At first there is a thinning of the foliage on the uppermost branches. As the years pass, the tree's crown becomes more and more transparent. Eventually dead branches can be seen projecting from the crown. Foliage thins out in the middle layers and more dead limbs appear. Finally branches break off and the whole tree may blow over in a storm.

Acid rain affects species throughout the ecosystem. Most insects, amphibians, and fish fail to reproduce when the pH of the water in which they live falls below 5.5. Blackflies are one exception. Blackflies

**POLLUTION FROM OHIO RIVER POWER PLANTS, SUCH AS THIS ONE, CONTRIBUTES TO ACID RAIN DAMAGE IN THE ADIRONDACKS.**

**CHAPEL POND IN THE ADIRONDACKS**

reproduce in greater numbers in areas that have acid water.

The New York Department of Environmental Conservation reports that acid rain is responsible for killing all fish in two hundred lakes at the highest elevations in the state. The acid in lake water leaches aluminum and other toxic metals from the rocks. Aluminum destroys the gills of fish. Unable to take in oxygen, the fish slowly suffocate. Twenty-five percent of Adirondack lakes have no fish, because the lakes are too acidic to support them. Higher-than-normal acid levels also kill amphibians' eggs and cause deformities in tadpoles.

Mercury is another toxic metal leached out of soil by acid. It is also found in the pollution smokestacks release into the atmosphere. Mercury kills fish and birds and is poisonous to humans. The New York Health Department has issued mercury warnings for more than one dozen lakes.

Each year more lakes and ponds become too acidic to support their natural life-forms. The Environmental Protection Agency predicts that 43 percent of all lakes and ponds in the Adirondacks will reach this critical point by the year 2040. These alarming statistics mean fewer insects, amphibians, and fish will live in the area, and less food will be available for birds and other secondary consumers. The food chain will break down, and the ecosystem will be threatened.

In 1990 Congress passed an amendment to the Clean Air Act that called for reductions in emissions of sulfur dioxide and nitrogen oxide by utility companies. Current scientific findings, however, make it clear that the problems have not been solved. In May 2001, a major conference in Washington, D.C., brought together scientists, economists, government leaders, public health officials, environmentalists, and ecologists to discuss the acid rain problem. One of their goals was to evaluate the effectiveness of the Clean Air Act. General findings from the conference showed that the United States has reduced sulfur dioxide and sulfur emissions. Acid rain is still a problem, though, because amounts of other pollutants in the environment, such as nitrogen oxide and ammonia, have increased.

**ENVIRONMENTAL ACTIVISTS TIED THIS PROTEST SIGN TO A LOG FOR A WASHINGTON, D.C., EARTH DAY EVENT IN APRIL 1990. THE U.S. CONGRESS PASSED AN IMPORTANT AMENDMENT TO THE CLEAN AIR ACT THAT YEAR.**

Ammonia comes from fertilizer spread on fields, automobiles' catalytic converters, power plants, sewage treatment plants, and animal waste. It acts as an acid when deposited on the earth's surface. Ironically, catalytic converters were placed on cars to control the amount of harmful compounds released into the air when automobiles burn gasoline. They have been successful in reducing some forms of air pollution, but recent studies have shown that they release high levels of ammonia gas and nitrous oxide as by-products in cars' exhaust. By fixing one pollution problem, another has been created.

Recommendations from the conference include reducing sulfur dioxide emissions by an additional 50 percent and nitrogen oxide by 60 percent. Nineteen states control nitrogen oxide emissions in the summer. Many feel controls are needed year-round and in all fifty states. Congress is discussing two bills that support legislation called the Acid Rain Control Act. If passed, it would further lower emission levels and

**AUTOMOBILE TRAFFIC CONTINUES TO POLLUTE THE ADIRONDACKS IN MANY WAYS.**

**WORKERS PLOW AND SPREAD SALT ON ICY ROADS FOR SAFE TRAVEL, BUT SALT IS HARMFUL TO TREES.**

regulate mercury emissions. Scientists predict that if sulfur dioxide is lowered by 80 percent, it will still take twenty-five years for soil to recover from the effects of acid rain. It's too soon to know what the long-term results will be, but public awareness and pollution controls are major steps in the right direction.

Trees are also susceptible to high levels of sodium in the soil. Sugar maples, in particular, are weakened and injured by salt added to road surfaces to melt ice and snow in the winter. The salt melts the ice and dissolves in the meltwater, which soaks into the ground. From there it enters the roots of trees. It is carried by the xylem to all parts of the trees. Eventually the trees die from high salt concentrations.

## LIFE IN THE ADIRONDACKS

The Adirondacks area is popular as an all-year sport and resort region. This has made tourism a major industry in the area, attracting people interested in hiking, camping, canoeing, and fishing.

Lumbering is mostly carried on by private landowners. The timber is used to manufacture furniture, paper, and building materials. Some iron ore, talc, and zinc are still mined on private lands.

Each spring maple producers in the Adirondacks make maple syrup, maple cream, and maple candy from the sap of sugar maple trees. As the soil warms and the sap rises, workers drill tap holes into the bark of sugar maples. They know how to

**HIKERS ENJOY FOLLOWING A STREAM IN THE ADIRONDACKS.**

tap the trees so minimal damage occurs, and the trees heal quickly. Sap is gathered in buckets or sent by plastic tubing to sugar houses, where it is boiled down to make maple syrup. Maple is also valued as a hardwood timber to make flooring, furniture, and cabinets. To many people, though, the sugar maple's greatest glory is apparent each autumn. That's when thousands of visitors come to the Adirondacks to see the tree's magnificent display of orange and red leaves.

Deciduous forests are essential to the long-term survival of our planet. They provide valuable resources, such as building materials and paper, for homes and businesses. They provide food in the form of nuts, berries, and maple syrup. They provide shelter for wildlife, protect and maintain the soil, keep the air and water clean, and help control global warming. For all of these reasons, we must work together to save our deciduous forests.

**BUCKETS FILL WITH SAP FROM MAPLE TREES (ACER) IN THE SPRING.**

# WHAT YOU CAN DO

Problems such as global warming and acid rain seem overwhelming. They appear to be too large for any one person to make a difference. If people took steps to reduce pollution in their home, school, and neighborhood, however, the overall effect would save trees, forests, and our planet.

Ways in which you can help include:

• Reduce waste to avoid creating pollution. Garbage dumps produce methane gas, one of the gases that cause the greenhouse effect. The average household in the United States produces at least 1 ton (1 metric ton) of trash each year.

• Reuse lunch bags, cloth napkins, plastic containers, and plastic bags.

• Walk, ride a bike, take the bus, or carpool. Limit use of all gasoline-powered vehicles and motors, such as cars, snowmobiles, outboard motors, lawnmowers, leaf blowers, and chainsaws.

• Use nontoxic products at home and school, such as nontoxic glue and markers for arts and crafts. Use baking soda, vinegar, and ordinary soap for household cleaning.

• Use cat litter or sand instead of chemicals or salt to melt ice on sidewalks.

• Avoid products containing mercury, such as fluorescent lamps, some medical equipment, and thermometers. Mercury is toxic to humans and wildlife.

• Use less paper and recycle what you do use. Forty percent of all garbage is paper. Americans throw away newsprint equal to thirty million trees each year. Recycling a stack of newspapers 3 feet (1 m) high saves one tree. Recycling 1 ton (1 metric ton) of paper

  – saves seventeen trees

  – reduces landfill space by 3.3 cubic yards (2.5 cubic m)

  – saves 7,100 gallons (27,000 liters) of water used in paper manufacturing, which is enough to supply the daily needs of thirty families

  – reduces energy use by 60 percent, saving 4,100 kilowatt-hours (15 gigajoules)

- Use less energy in order to decrease the amount of carbon dioxide going into the atmosphere from power-generating plants.
  - Turn off lights when leaving a room. One-fourth of the energy generated in the United States is used for lighting.
  - Switch off electronic equipment, such as televisions, VCRs, music systems, and computers. Don't put them on standby.
  - Turn off water while brushing your teeth.
  - Run full loads in the washing machine and dishwasher.
- Stay informed about what your school, neighborhood, community, and city are doing to reduce waste and pollution.
- Write letters to government officials asking for stricter controls on air quality and pollution.

**To write to the president:**

The President
The White House
Washington, D.C. 20500

**To write to the senators from your state:**

The Honorable (name of your senator)
United States Senate
Washington, D.C. 20510

**To write to your representative in Congress:**

The Honorable (name of your representative)
U.S. House of Representatives
Washington, D.C. 20515

# WEBSITES TO VISIT FOR MORE INFORMATION

The following websites contain a wealth of information. All suggest further web links for more information.

## The Adirondacks: A Gift of Wilderness

<http://www.northnet.org/adirondackvic/about.html>
This website contains information about the Adirondack Park prepared by the Adirondack Park Visitor Interpretive Centers in Paul Smiths and Newcomb, NY.

## Clean Air–Cool Planet (CA–CP)

<http://www.cleanair-coolplanet.org>
CA–CP's goal is to reduce greenhouse gas emissions in the northeastern United States. It reports on current climatic problems and presents suggestions for change.

## Global Warming

<http://yosemite.epa.gov/oar/globalwarming.nsf/content/index.html>
This United States Environmental Protection Agency site has information about how individuals can make a difference in reducing global warming. It links to other energy sites.

## High Peaks Wilderness Area

<http://www.dec.state.ny.us/website/dlf/publands/adk/index.html>
This page provides information from the New York State Department of Environmental Conservation about the Adirondack Forest Preserve, including its history, wildlife, trails, and environmental concerns.

## New York State Department of Environmental Conservation

<http://www.dec.state.ny.us>
The home page of the New York State Department of Environmental Conservation has regulations and

policies for environmental protection of air and water, plus other information about conservation, wildlife, and forests.

**World Wildlife Fund**
<http://www.worldwildlife.org>
This website provides information about climate change and global warming, forests, toxic chemicals, and endangered species. The World Wildlife Fund is dedicated to protecting the world's wildlife and wildlands.

# FOR FURTHER READING

Johnson, Rebecca L. *The Greenhouse Effect.* Minneapolis, MN: Lerner Publications Company, 1990.

Kalinowski, Tom. *Adirondack Almanac: A Guide to the Natural Year.* Utica, NY: North Country Books, 1999.

Kaplan, Elizabeth. *Temperate Forest.* New York: Benchmark Books, 1996.

Ketchledge, E. H. *Forests and Trees of the Adirondack High Peaks Region.* Lake George, NY: Adirondack Mountain Club, 1996.

Madgwick, Wendy. *Fungi and Lichens.* Austin, TX: Steck-Vaughn, 1990.

McClung, Robert M. *Lost Wild America: The Story of Our Extinct and Vanishing Wildlife.* Hamden, CT: Linnet Books, 1993.

Patent, Dorothy Hinshaw. *Biodiversity.* New York: Clarion Books, 1996.

Sayre, April Pulley. *Temperate Deciduous Forest.* New York: Twenty-First Century Books, 1994.

Scott, Michael. *Ecology.* New York: Oxford University Press, 1995.

Swinburne, Stephen R. *Coyote.* Honesdale, PA: Boyd's Mill Press, 1999.

VanCleave, Janice. *Ecology for Every Kid: Easy Activities That Make Learning About Science Fun.* New York: John Wiley & Sons, 1996.

Whitman, Sylvia. *This Land Is Your Land: The American Conservation Movement.* Minneapolis, MN: Lerner Publications Company, 1994.

# GLOSSARY

**abiotic:** nonliving. The nonliving, physical parts of an ecosystem include minerals, nutrients, the temperature, and precipitation.

**abscission layer:** a layer of cells at the base of each deciduous leaf stem. In the fall, it cuts off nutrients to the leaf.

**acid:** a compound that contains hydrogen and has a pH of less than 7

**acid rain:** rain that contains acid from pollution in the air

**alternation of generations:** a system of reproduction in which a spore-producing generation of plants alternates with a generation that produces sex cells

**biome:** a particular type of living community of plants and animals, such as may be found in deciduous forests or deserts

**biotic:** living. The living parts of an ecosystem include plants, animals, fungi, and bacteria.

**cambium:** a layer of soft tissue between the wood and the bark of a tree, from which new wood and bark grow

**canopy:** the uppermost branchy layer of a forest, or its tallest treetops

**carnivore:** a meat-eating animal

**catalytic converter:** a device placed on cars that converts harmful compounds in car exhaust into less harmful ones

**chlorophyll:** the green pigment found in plants that makes photosynthesis possible

**clear-cutting:** cutting all of the trees in an area of land

**climax forest:** a forest that has reached a stable, self-sustaining, long-lasting balance with its environment

**conifer:** a tree that bears its seeds in cones

**deciduous trees:** trees that shed their leaves each fall

**decomposers:** organisms, such as bacteria and fungi, that break down plant and animal remains into nutrients that plants can use

**ecosystem:** a specific community of plants, animals, and other living organisms, and their nonliving environment

**ephemerals:** flowers that bloom for short

periods of time early in the spring, before the forest's canopy fills with leaves

**food chain:** the transfer of energy from plants to animals as each eats and is eaten

**fruiting body:** the part of a fungus that makes spores

**gametes:** male and female sex cells

**gametophyte:** the stage in a fern's life cycle that produces male and female sex cells

**gestation:** the period of development before birth

**global warming:** an increase in the earth's temperature due to an increase in gases that insulate the earth

**greenhouse effect:** The trapping of heat near the earth's surface by gases

**heartwood:** wood found in the center of a tree's trunk that gives the tree rigidity

**herbivore:** a plant-eating animal

**herb layer:** the layer of soft-stemmed plants growing close to the forest floor

**humus:** a layer of decomposed organic material in the soil

**hypha (pl. hyphae):** a thread that makes up the mycelium of a fungus

**intolerant species:** species of plants that grow in open areas with lots of sunshine

**invertebrate:** an animal without a backbone

**mycelium:** a mass of interwoven threads that make up the main part of a fungus

**mycorrhizal relationship:** the mutually beneficial relationship between tree roots and their fungus partners

**old growth forests:** forests with trees that have lived three hundred years or more

**omnivore:** an animal that eats both plants and animals

**parasite:** an organism that depends for its existence on living plants or animals

**perennial:** a plant that lives for more than one year

**phloem:** the layer of a tree's trunk that transports food from the leaves

**photosynthesis:** the process by which green plants use sunlight and chlorophyll to convert carbon dioxide and water into sugar

**pioneer species:** the first plants that grow in an area after a disturbance, such as a fire

**predator:** an animal that hunts and eats other animals

**primary consumer:** an animal that eats plants

**primary producer:** a green plant that makes its own food

**prothallus:** a small heart-shaped plant that produces the sex cells from which a fern grows

**rhizoids:** rootlike threads that anchor mosses or liverworts to the surface upon which they grow

**rhizomes:** stems of ferns that are usually underground

**saprophyte:** an organism that feeds on decaying plant or animal remains

**sapwood:** the part of a tree's trunk through which water and minerals move from the roots to the leaves; also called xylem

**scavenger:** an animal that eats the remains of dead animals

**seed-tree cutting:** a method of harvesting trees. Several large trees are left to provide a seed source for new growth.

**shelterwood cutting:** a method of harvesting trees. Some trees are left standing to provide a partial canopy.

**snag:** a standing dead tree

**spore:** a single cell from which mosses, lichens, ferns, or fungi grow

**sporophyte:** the generation of a fern plant that produces spores

**succession:** the process by which plant communities replace one another

**symbiosis:** a mutually beneficial relationship between two different organisms

**till:** glacial debris ranging in size from tiny particles of clay and silt to large rocks and boulders

**tolerant species:** species able to grow in full shade

**torpor:** a sluggish state in which an animal's body temperature and functions are greatly reduced during cold winter months

**transitional forests:** forests with tree varieties from two adjoining ecosystems

**understory:** the middle layer of a forest that includes smaller trees and the trunks of large trees

**xylem:** the part of the tree's trunk that carries water and minerals from the roots to all parts of the tree; also called sapwood

# INDEX

# ABOUT THE AUTHOR

Dianne M. MacMillan loves hiking in the woods. She believes that an understanding of the life cycle of our forests is vital to preserving our wilderness areas for future generations. The deciduous forests of the Adirondacks are a peek into what our country's landscape was like when the first colonists arrived. Ms. MacMillan hopes that this book will be a window to the future so that the diversity of wildlife and plants will continue to be protected and cherished, thereby ensuring the future health of our planet.

Ms. MacMillan, a former elementary school teacher, is an accomplished author who has published both fiction and nonfiction children's books. She regularly visits classrooms to talk with young people about her writing experiences. Previous Lerner Publications titles are *Missions of the Los Angeles Area* and *Destination Los Angeles*. She has also written two Carolrhoda Nature Watch books, *Elephants: Our Last Land Giants* and *Cheetahs*. Ms. MacMillan lives in Anaheim Hills, California, with her husband and youngest daughter.

# PHOTO ACKNOWLEDGEMENTS

© Gerry Lemmo, pp. 2–3, 8 (left), 16 (both), 27 (left), 28 (right), 29, 30 (bottom), 35 (right), 37 (right), 39, 45 (right), 46, 47, 48, 61, 62, 63; © Catherine Gehm, pp. 8 (right); © Tom Till, p. 9; © A. Gurmankin/Visuals Unlimited, p. 11; © Bill Beatty, pp. 13, 23, 27 (right bottom), 30 (top), 31 (right), 45 (left bottom); © Kent & Donna Dannen, pp. 17, 22, 37 (left bottom), 57; © Rob Curtis/ The Early Birder, pp. 21 (left), 40 (top left and bottom left), 54 © Todd Fink/Daybreak Imagery, p. 21 (right); © Susan Day/Daybreak Imagery, p. 27 (right top); © Richard Day/Daybreak Imagery, pp. 28 (left), 31 (left); © Mark & Sue Werner/The Image Finders, pp. 32, 40 (right), 49 (top); © Jim Hamilton, p. 33; © Rob Curtis/ The Early Birder/ The Image Finders, p. 35 (left); © Paul M. Butler/The Image Finders, p. 37 (left top), 45 (left top); © Gerard Fuehrer/ Visuals Unlimited, p. 41; © Tom Uhlman/The Image Finders, p. 42; © Kenny Bahr/The Image Finders, p. 49 (bottom); North Wind Picture Archives, p. 50; © Patti McConville/The Image Finders, p. 58; Todd Gipstein/ CORBIS, p. 59; © Steve Callahan/Visuals Unlimited, p. 60 (left); © Reuters NewMedia Inc./CORBIS, p. 60 (right). Map and illustrations on pp. 10, 15, 19, 26 by Bill Hauser. Bottom border, Corbis Royalty Free. Cover: © Gerry Lemmo